THE AUTHENTIC LEADER AS SERVANT (ALS)

ALS II COURSE 5
INITIATION LEADERSHIP
Attributes, Principles, and Practices

SYLVANUS N. WOSU, Ph.D

THE AUTHENTIC LEADER AS SERVANT
ALS II COURSE 5
Developing Initiative Leadership Attributes, Principles, and Practices

© Copyright 2024 by Sylvanus N. Wosu Ph.D.

Printed in the United States of America
ISBN: 978-1-959449-90-4

All rights reserved. No part of this book may be reproduced or transmitted in any form or by any means, electronic or mechanical, including photocopying, recording, or by any information storage and retrieval system, without permission in writing from the copyright owner.

Bible quotations are from the New King James (NKJV) version of the Bible unless otherwise indicated.

Other versions used in this book are the New International Version (NIV), New Living Translation (NLT), King James Version (KJV), English Standard Version (ESV), and Good News Translation (GNT). Unless otherwise specified, NKJV should be assumed.

The views expressed in this work are solely those of the author and do not necessarily reflect the views of the publisher, and the publisher disclaims any responsibility for them.

To order additional copies of this book, contact:
Proisle Publishing Services LLC
39-67 58th Street, 1st floor
Woodside, NY 11377, USA
Phone: (+1 646-480-0129)
info@proislepublishing.com

PROISLE PUBLISHING

TABLE OF CONTENTS

FOREWORD — XI
ACKNOWLEDGMENTS — XV
DEDICATION — XVII
PREFACE — 19
    About Leader As Servant Leadership (LSL) Model — 22
    About the Authentic Leader as Servant (ALS) — 25
    About the ALS Courses — 26

CHAPTER 1
UNDERSTANDING LEADERSHIP ATTRIBUTES — 35
    Functional Definitions — 35
    Comparisons With Other Works — 40
    Principle of Leadership Attribute — 42
    Authentic Leadership Attributes — 43
    Summary 1 Understanding Leadership Process — 48

CHAPTER 2
INITIATION LEADERSHIP ATTRIBUTE — 51
    Servant Leadership Initiative Attribute — 51
    Principle of Leadership Initiative Attribute — 52
    Summary 2 Initiative Leadership Attribute — 53

CHAPTER 3
DEVELOPING INITIATION-VISION — 57
    Foresighted with the Correct Perspective — 58
    Being Courageous to Initiate — 59
    Summary 3 Developing Initiation-Vision — 60

CHAPTER 4
DEVELOPING INITIATION-INFLUENCE — 63
    Influence Buy-In For Action by Inspiration — 63
    Influence by Decisive Conviction — 63
    Influence by an Outward Commitment — 64
    Summary 4 Developing Initiation-Influence — 64

CHAPTER 5
DEVELOPING INITIATION-FOCUS 67

Focus on Your Vision–Purpose -- 67
Focus with a passion to complete the process --- 67
Focus spiritually to act on the initiation --- 68
Summary 5 Developing the Initiation-Focus --- 68

CHAPTER 6
DEVELOPING INITIATION- ACTION 71

A Case of Initiating a Process of Change --- 71
A Case of Initiating a Desired Change -- 74
Summary 6 Developing the Initiation-Action -------------------------------------- 77

TOPIC INDEX 79
REFERENCES 81

FOREWORD

The modern world today is obsessed with standardization and modalities. As a result, in the realm of leadership, many books have spout associated leadership theories and models and explain them as the path to follow. However, the critical dimensions that distinguish the effectiveness of any leadership process are the values and attribute the leader brings to the table; desired change is influenced by leadership styles or standards. These many standards and theories of leadership often are not in step with the changing times or the followers' needs. The trend is a bit like stocking different kinds of foods in a grocery store and expecting that they will meet everybody's needs the same way and at all times. Aisles are packed with varieties of food with expiration dates in the future, but getting the best deal on the products is what really matters to those who buy and use the products

In many ways, this is the state of leadership in the modern world. Increasingly, even leaders of public institutions are tasked with turning a profit for themselves or the organization they serve. The idea of a "leader" seems to float uneasily alongside the ranks of fundraisers or profit raisers in contrast to any kind of role model for followers or employees. That which is knowable, measurable, and marketable has surpassed the difficult intangibility of strong moral leadership attributes as the central guideline for achievement and success.

In this complicated space, Dr. Sylvanus Wosu introduces his complex idea of the Leader as a Servant Leadership, which is in this book, modeled on Christian tradition. Like all intricate ideas, Dr. Wosu's central point depends on a paradox: a person is best qualified to lead when he or she is most ready to serve. This paradox has been monopolized rhetorically by "public servants" who often serve either self-interest or the interests of specific lobbies. The Authentic Leader as Servant penetrates past the superficial concept of "serving" and details the internal state of true servitude or Servanthood.

While the book is primarily focused on the Christian model of leadership attributes such as discipleship, empathy, affection, and Servanthood, it does so not merely on the grounds of blind faith, but rather via numerous contemporary sociological and business-driven studies on how leaders should seek a leader-follower relationship that is simultaneously productive and nurturing. Dr. Wosu's most piercing insights always involve this secular–Christian dialogue. This book demonstrates that Christ's model for leadership is one that may exist successfully outside the confines of a faith relationship; it places the values of Christ's religious significance in leadership at the center of the framework. It is clear from Dr. Wosu's generous own life story of faith—a faith tested by humbling difficulties—is at the center of both his orientation and motivation for writing.

In language that is so concise, it is often illustrated in mathematical formulas; Dr. Wosu explains the deep structural integrity of Christ's Leader as the Servant Leadership model. One could imagine leaders of any doctrine benefiting from the analyses contained in these pages. The book's message repeatedly encourages the reader to imagine a scenario or reflect on memories and personal experiences to prove or test its many points. Thus, the book depends on a form of praxis, a lesson that could be or has been enacted, by the participating reader. I am very impressed at the volume and level of thinking of the author. Parts of the book involve his personal story, which is especially riveting. I cannot imagine what he had to endure, which he referred to as a" wilderness walk," to accomplish the goal he set for himself. His life stories on these pages are inspiring and stimulating.

In this way, the text eschews dogmatism in favor of the self-discovery Socratic Method of teaching and learning. The reader is not badgered into complying with a religious objective but is rather asked to consider the applicability of difficult biblical concepts in relation to modern life. It is a fascinating and very thought-provoking read.

Hence, the book does not seek to make the leader a servant, a cookie-cutter corporate buzzword, but rather asks the reader to imagine him or herself interacting with a range of concepts. One of Dr. Wosu's great strengths is his reservation when it comes to forcing his reading's interpretation on the material he presents.

The book parallels Biblical and modern leadership scenarios in ways that consistently provoke thought, and while it is clear Dr. Wosu has his particular leadership style; the space for the reader's own thoughts is always left open.

The book could not have been written in any other way with integrity. Its format and formulas are offered to the reader of the leader as a servant role that it analyzes in its pages. To find a text that instructs from this humble position is profoundly refreshing in a genre that is often packaged inside a cover with a sizeable picture of the "modest" author, smiling egotistically beneath a name spelled out in large, gold lettering. Throughout its pages, this text feels as if it serves the reader.

In the end, this is the most satisfying aspect of the book. There is no standardized approach to achieving successful leadership. There is no promise of power and a bigger payday; in fact, the book often proffers just the opposite. The reader is not encouraged to devalue the experience of leadership by finding some economic metric for marking success but is rather asked to think deeply about the most basic elements of internal and social interaction within the framework of a Christian tradition. What this means will be different for every reader. Indeed, even in the context of single chapters, I found myself questioning or re-evaluating moments of my own life. This book serves; it doesn't feel like filling in multiple-choice questions, staring at a wall of flavorless grocery products, or hearing the endless servant promises of today's political scene. It feels like a humble invitation to consider a single paradoxical element of a profoundly productive tradition.

-Tobias Bates

Acknowledgments

A book on leadership attributes as aspects of Servant Leadership sprouted from the wealth of knowledge and the inspirations of many other leaders. Their writings were sources of inspiration, challenges, and examples of excellence to emulate. I acknowledge the leaders listed below for their help in one way or the other. I am very grateful and I hereby express my appreciation and thanks:

Mr. Wayne Holt, introduced me first to the subject of Servanthood in one of our Stephen Ministerial Training classes, and he is the one who has conducted his life as a leader–servant; he encouraged me throughout my writing;

Dr. Harvey Borovetz, Distinguished Professor and Chair of the Bioengineering Department, is a leader-servant in many ways, he modeled Servanthood and encouragement attributes throughout his leadership in an academic setting.

Dr. Clifford and Dr. Patience Obih, in so many measures exemplified the practical leadership attributes discussed in this book.

Pastor Lance Lecocq, Lead Pastor of Monroeville Assembly of God, for his excellent model of servanthood, empowerment, and emulation attributes to the ministerial team, I am thankful for his motivation and encouragement throughout the several hours on this project;

To my administrative assistant, Ms. Terri Cook, who was always the first to review the manuscript; I am very grateful for her dedication.

To the African Christian Fellowship USA, institutions, and all other organizations where I have served in one leadership capacity or the other, thank you for affording me senior leadership positions that provided the leadership platform and opportunities to grow as a leader.

Dr. Lawrence Owoputi, a brother I am proud to call my friend; for his dedication to serving others, his generosity, healing care, and responsibility attributes during our term in office and in chapter leadership positions; he taught me that excellent following is also part of good leadership;

To Tobias Bates, for his editorial work on the original draft of the book, and his dedication to completing the work.

Mr. Edward F. Kondis, a member of our Engineering Board of Visitors, for his always encouraging and moral support;

Dr. Enefaa N. Wosu, my wife and life partner, for her love, commitment, and prayer support, especially during those long night hours I was not there for her and her constant reminder of who I must be as a leader-servant. Without her support, forbearance, wisdom, and encouragement, this project would not have been completed; I say, thank you very much.

And to God alone be all the glory and honor for the divine inspiration and guidance in initiating and completing this life-transforming book project.

Dedication

I humbly submit this book back unto the gracious hands of God who inspired the writings through His Holy Spirit!

I dedicate this book to my virtuous wife of 45 years, Rev. (Dr.) Enefaa Wosu whose spiritual leadership is an important gateway to our home, and to our four wonderful children—Prof. Eliada Wosu-Griffin EL, HeCareth, Tamuno-Emi, and Chidinma. From them all, I learnt what it meant to be a leader-servant. I could not be blessed with better teachers.

PREFACE

What characteristics did Biblical leaders like the Apostle Paul, Moses, Joshua, and Nehemiah as servants of their people display outwardly that distinguished them from other leaders, both then and now? The Apostle Paul kept his focus to *emulate* Christ and endured all the infirmities and persecutions he suffered to complete his goal to preach the gospel of Jesus Christ. He inspired Timothy and others through his effective *discipleship* leadership to imitate him as he emulated Christ. Moses' outward display of his *trust* in God's power earned him a good level of trust from the people and empowered him for the mission of delivery of God's children from bondage in Egypt; he had to *reproduce* himself in Joshua to complete the mission. But the greatest of them was Jesus Christ, who humbly sacrificed His life to finish the work of redemption. In His *Servanthood*, commitment, and love for the people, He became the ultimate *model* of a leader as a servant to *emulate*.

Let's consider for a moment secular leaders in these current times! For example, think of Henry Ford, who founded the successful Ford Motor Company; Bill Gates who created the global empire that is Microsoft; Albert Einstein, who in many ways is synonymous with a genius for his contributions to modern physics; Abraham Lincoln, remembered as one of the greatest presidents and leaders of United States; and many others like these we cannot mention. What did all these leaders have in common? What propelled them to turn their initial failures or challenges into eventual successes? None had a direct mentor or inherited any fortune from their parents. Nevertheless, they all eventually succeeded. These people can be distinguished from others based on their self-will to succeed, their self-confidence and belief in themselves, their self-determination, and their perseverance, among other characteristics. The distinguishing characteristics displayed externally in service or relationships toward others are the outward functional attributes that define that leader.

Think about yourself as a student, faculty member, or that new executive. What was it that made your journey to success different and even great? Students and colleagues, when they see or hear about my display of what I have referred to as the 'wilderness walk of faith', have asked me to share the critical attitudinal elements that made me remain inwardly resilient and undaunted and yet outwardly joyful in the difficulties I had faced. This book is the result of those reflections. Let me explain one such teaching moment.

Many years ago, sitting in my research lab on a Saturday morning trying to finish writing my dissertation, a fellow graduate student walked into the room to talk with me. He was contemplating terminating his graduate studies. He was a privileged single male student but felt the load was just too much.

"Sylvanus," he asked, with seriousness in his eyes, "your research advisor suggested that I should ask you, 'what is it that makes you tick?'.'What is it about you' that makes you joyful and at peace with yourself and determined to finish, no matter the situations and high expectations we face in this department?"

What he asked me were deeply reflective questions, but I was willing and excited to answer them. Even so, before I do, let's look at the context. At that period in my life, I had four little children as a graduate student; in fact, more children than any of the faculties at that time, except for one faculty member who had eight children. I received little or no support from the department. I was then an international alien, did not qualify for financial aid, and was not given any research assistant position. I was, therefore, self-supported with two off-campus part-time jobs. I joked at being a minority of minorities, the only student in the department with such a label,—but I was self-willed to succeed. My adaptability attribute, coupled with perseverance and resilience, was all that I needed to succeed despite the odds against me. In every exam, homework assignment, or project I had to compete with students with full financial aid, plus they had nothing to distract their attention from their studies. I lived with the attitude that using disadvantages as an excuse was not an option. Aspiring to earn my Ph.D. was a life dream, and I was willing to give my ultimate best to actualize that dream even in the face of challenges. The choice was mine!

So I looked at my classmate and all I could see was a student striding through a valley through which I also walked. He needed me to show him how to walk the walk, to empathize with him. To answer his question, I smiled, not that I wanted to, but because it was just who I was. The joy he attributed to me was an overflow of my appreciation of God's grace that His life in me was externally manifesting His light to bless someone else. It was a great teaching moment; I capitalized on it to tell my classmate that my joy was not about me. He could see physically but about He who was in me, he could not see in the flesh; I needed him to know that I was just showing forth His life in me. At first, my classmate did not understand the spiritual prose or metaphor I was using. He looked surprised but open to hearing more.

I did not ask if he was a Christian. However, right on my desk was my small green pocket Bible. I opened to 2 Corinthians 12:9 (NIV) and handed it to him to read. As he read the passage: "But he said to me, 'My grace is sufficient for you, for my power is made perfect in weakness.' Therefore, I will boast all the more gladly about my weaknesses, so that Christ's power may rest on me," I noticed how absorbed he was in the words

He looked astonished and read it again, this time silently. "This is interesting, but what does this mean?" He asked. I took his question to mean, "How does this relate to my question?

I explained to my friend that the external attitudes he or my advisors saw in me that warranted the question, "What makes you tick" were inspired by my inner value system based on my faith in this same Christ and His teachings. My desire to manifest His life and self-confidence is all because of what He has promised in His word if I believed. I have believed His words and have gained self-determination and faith to make the right choices through Him for my life, and his spirit has given me perseverance and resilience to focus on finishing strong in pursuit of any goal. "With that faith, I have continued, more passionately and excitedly; I can look at my challenges and vulnerabilities and delight joyfully in them, even as an alien minority of minorities! His grace and power have empowered me to do all things I want to do. That is what makes me tick," I explained.

He looked at me as if he got his answer. "Wow, thanks!" he said, looking inspired and ready to face his challenges. As we concluded with a prayer, and he stood up to leave, I pointed empathetically to his face and said, "If I made it despite my challenges, you have absolutely no excuse but to persevere to complete your studies; you can make it too!"

It is fitting to report that this encounter with my classmate transformed his will and determination to continue. Yes, he was encouraged and went on to complete his graduate studies. He emulated self-will and perseverance from the example of the most vulnerable of all students in the department.

The inner value system of a Leader-Servant is founded not only on his faith but his self-will, coupled with self-leadership; it is the greatest mentor who can turn any situation into an inconceivable success. Self-will is the primary driver for determination, resilience, and perseverance. It is what wakes you up in the morning to ask for strength to do whatever it is you are setting out to do. Based on my life walk of faith, I can state with absolute certainty that faith is the unseen assuredness that can empower you to turn your life's probable impossibilities into great and improbable possibilities.

ABOUT LEADER AS SERVANT LEADERSHIP (LSL) MODEL

Looking at the testimony above, do you know the source that energizes the characteristics you display outside and how your inner self is related to what others see outside? What distinguishes you from others is what combines to define your attributes! As a follower, can you identify the characteristics that distinguish your leaders? As an executive, how do you base your evaluation of yourself? Or how do you evaluate that brand-new manager or new youth director you want to hire? To what do you compare the individual's qualities when you look at his CV? What is the basis of your measure? Do you know if you are a substantial leader? These personal questions and much more are the subjects of this two-volume book, 'The Authentic Leader as Servant Part I: The Outward Leadership Attributes, Principles, and Practices', is written in two parts; the second part 'The Leader as Servant Leadership Model. Part II'; deals with the Inner Strength Leadership Attributes, Principles, and Practices.

When we think about today's corporate greed, deepening divide between the haves and have-not, gridlock in political systems, conflicts and wars, high divorce rates, and the rich young ruler in the Bible, it is easy to agree that all these people share a few things in common: self-centeredness, pride, lack of compassion, and greed. There is a great need in today's suffering world for leader-servants who display leadership attributes. These attributes should be oriented toward selfless service to others. Indeed, our world is increasingly drifting away from global serving reality toward the self and apathy. The most credible message or model for a possible solution to this dilemma and the answer to several complex leadership questions can be found in the foundation of the ultimate leader-servant, Jesus Christ. This book defines the Leader as Servant Leadership attribute as the combined acts of two or more distinctive functional leadership characteristics exhibited in service and relationship toward others. There is no better time than now for a book that presents comprehensive and irrevocable facts and principles regarding how to develop effective attributes of the leader-servant.

The Leader as Servant Leadership Model

My first book on this subject, The Leader as Servant Leadership Model, explains that Jesus' servant leadership model is based on the notion of a Leader as a Servant and not on a Servant as Leader. There are four distinct differences between a Servant as Leader (Servant-leader) and the Leader as Servant (leader--servant) models. It is pertinent to highlight them here to connect to this book, Authentic Leader as Servant.

A Leader as Servant is a leader first. The leader–servant as a leader does not in the line of duty go projecting or lording his or her power and authority over others but is the person to lead the process of influencing desired changes in others through his humble example of being a servant or having a serviceable attitude toward others. He or she is a serving leader, not a lording leader. He leads as a servant by putting others' needs above his own needs and rights. Jesus emphasized the word "as" meaning that the leader (the Master) chooses to serve as a servant even though he is the leader. A leader–servant emulates Jesus, who gave up all rights, and emptied and expended Himself on His followers. He empowered them to become more like Him. A leader-servant is known as a leader first but is seen as a great leader by his humble attendant heart and acts of service to others. His greatness comes from his ability to put others above himself.

Leader as Servant is a Biblical Concept. The model or image of a humble serving leader motivated Jesus' disciples to see that if their master could do this for them, they must also be able to do it for others. Jesus clearly demonstrated the process of leader-as-servant leadership. In some cases, He chose to serve by leading when He wanted to create the image or model of the leader-servant in certain acts. In other cases, He chose to lead by serving, when he showed care and empathy toward the people and led the disciples to see empathy as a leadership attribute.

Leader as Servant is an Authentic Leadership Model to follow. The Leader as the Servant leadership model intentionally positions Jesus as an original model of a leader to follow.

He was serving His disciples to demonstrate that the process of becoming a great leader was earned through humble acts of service to others; He made them understand that He was empowering them to succeed Him as leader-servants through service to others. The result was an incomparable legacy of leadership that changed their communities. The fact that Jesus relinquished his rights or shared His power did not diminish His power and influence. In fact, his influence increased at least 11 X 100%, if we ignore the one case of Judas.

The Leader as Servant Transforms Organizational Culture. The proposed LSL model seeks to transform and sustain the community or organization by instilling key leadership values or "leadership presence" among followers or an organization's members. Change is sustained when everyone in the organization takes ownership of the change. Rather than focusing on leading more followers to be great followers who conform to the organizational culture, LSL seeks to lead and empower better leaders to be distinguished leaders and community builders.

There are four distinctions, which clearly differentiate many of the existing servants as Leader-based philosophies in relation to servant leadership from my LSL model. Even in the corporate or institutional worlds, there is nothing better than Jesus on which to base Servant Leadership. There is nothing more authentic and impacting than the servant leadership modeled by the life and teachings of Jesus Christ.

The LSL model uses exploratory questions, scenarios, and graphic visualizations to excite critical thinking in ways no other book on this subject has yet attempted. Several personal testimonies of my wilderness walk of faith with God are used to connect the reader to real-life experiences of the concepts discussed. The riveting effect is that the text engages and encourages the reader to walk through the experiences presented. The aim is to inspire the reader spiritually, mentally, and professionally with this far-reaching exposition on the subject of servant leadership.

ABOUT THE AUTHENTIC LEADER AS SERVANT (ALS)

The *Authentic Leader as Servant* argues that no leadership model is as authentic, other-centered, able to build communities, and productive and service-oriented as the model of our ultimate leader-servant, Jesus Christ. No source can provide a better point of reference than that provided in the Bible. Hence, this book aims to be more than just a text on leadership; it hopes to be a personal discovery for those who aspire to develop effective leadership attributes that grow leaders as servants who ultimately develop thriving other-centered communities. This book presents a comprehensive, biblically-based study regarding how to develop these attributes and how they are applied in a servant leadership process. In this biblical context and for clarity, Servant Leadership means *Leader-as-Servant Leadership*. A *leader-servant* refers to a *leader as a servant*, which is distinct from a servant-leader or servant as leader.

Leader as Servant Leadership attributes are shaped by the Leadership's Inner Value system, which consists of character, motivation, and commitment. The *Authentic Leader as Servant* is presented as a necessary resource to complement my *The Leader as Servant Leadership (LSL) Model*. The LSL model integrates a transformative leadership framework and interactive dimensions of Servant Leadership. Leader as Servant Leadership is a process in which a leader, in his leadership position, purposefully chooses to put others' rights and needs above his positional rights and personal needs. He then serves, enables, and empowers followers for growth that builds a thriving organization. The LSL model looks at the predominant Servant Leadership concepts and shares how they compare with biblical principles on how we should lead and be led.

ABOUT THE ALS COURSES

The three books, *LSL Model* and *The Authentic Leader as Servant* (Parts I and II), together demonstrate that with today's global visions to reach people of all races and cultures, now is the time for an authentic servant's heart of service. Those visions and the leadership processes are most effective with the appropriate leadership attributes centered more on people than on the organization, principles regarding how to develop effective attributes of leader-servant.

The ALS I and II combined presented twenty leaders as servant leadership attributes. The series of ALS courses supply training guide to understand, develop, and practice the attributes in a leadership process. Each course is independent and self-contained and does not depend on completing any other course in the series of 20 courses. It is, however strongly recommended, in fact a must read, that chapters 1 and 2 in each series be covered as they lay the foundation of LSL model on which ALS is based.

ALS (Parts I & II) Course Layout

The *Authentic Leader as Servant (ALS)* leadership (parts I and II) book has been broken down into 20 courses in workbook format to achieve three goals 1) Self-discovery of the acts of developing the attribute under review in the course, 2) deeper understanding of the principles, research and biblical teaching behind the attributes, and 3) Learning the strategies for practicing the attributes.

Instruction

The set of questions following each chapter are designed to serve as a guide to discover, explore, and practice the essential ALS leadership attributes, principles, and practices in leadership process. The questions are comprehensive review based on the content of this specific chapter only.

To maximize the learning outcomes, the learner must read through this chapter and sections. Some referenced scriptures in the book are repeated in the summaries for added review if needed, even though they were discussed in the section in which they apply.

> The exercises that follow each chapter will help you in not only understanding your own strength and weaknesses in your acts of the attribute but will guide you in developing practical strategies you can apply in self-leadership process or helping others grow in leadership
>
> All answers to the questions are contained in the associated chapter or sections; consultation of new sources, except for the reference scriptures, is not needed. Thus, it is expected that you answer the questions after you have read the associated section or chapter of the workbook. The scripture or other references cited are only for references as they already discussed in the book

ALS II Course 1: Adaptability Leadership Attribute—*Flexibility overcomes rigidity in new and changing situations.*

Adaptability is framed as an inner strength quality of a leader in responding to changing needs or situations in a service mission. According to the Army training Handbook, adaptability is "an individual's ability to recognize changes in the environment, identify the critical elements of the new situation, and trigger changes accordingly to meet new requirements." God showed Moses adaptability when he empowered him to use the rod in his hand as an instrument for the mission ahead of him. This course will attempt to give meanings to personal reflective questions to discover the distinguishing characteristics of Leadership Adaptability. Numerous techniques, personal examples, empirical case studies, and applications of the adaptability developing strategies are discussed concepts. Practice questions at the end of each chapter are used to guide your development and to frame meanings out of the content to improve your acts of adaptability in a leadership process.

ALS II Course 2: Courage Leadership Attribute—*Courage is the inner strength of the mind to triumph over paralyzing fears of purposeful action that yields good success*

Courage Leadership Attribute is the lynchpin of effective Servant Leadership that supports the display of all the other attributes? Having the inner strength of character and convictions to persevere and hold on to new and often misunderstood ideas in the face of opposition takes courage—inner strength to triumph over the fear of failure or danger. It is even greater courage to venture into positions or overcome situations that nobody like you, has gone to before or where many better qualified than you had gone and failed. In all cases, they all display courage in the face of obstacles and uncertainties. The success is more about courage than the experience. Can such courage be learned or inspired? How do leaders or successful people in their callings get to their heights of achievements? How can courage be an inner strength within or beyond leadership? How does courage attribute triumph over paralyzing fear? This course explores answers to these questions and more by searching for the distinguishing characteristics of courage. Numerous techniques, personal examples, empirical case studies, including practice questions at the end of each chapter are used to guide your development and to frame meanings out of the content to improve your acts of courage leadership process.

ALS II Course 3: Empathy Leadership Attribute—*A measure of a leader's compassion is the empathic engagement in a follower's experience and state of well-being beyond just expressions of feelings and concerns.*

Empathy attribute is the ability to project one's personality and experiences into another person's thoughts, emotions, direct experience, position, and act toward the wellness of that person. How can a leader walk along with someone in that individual's "wilderness" state of suffering or danger? What motivates a leader to *empathize* with a follower? How is empathy an inner strength leadership attribute? Whether it's in your church, your business, your institution, or in your community, this course provides a comprehensive biblical-based discussion on the role of a leader as a servant in empathizing with those he leads. The aim is to inspire the reader spiritually, mentally, and professionally with this far-reaching exposition on empathy in servant leadership. How can a leader make a lasting positive impact in the lives of those he or she leads? Answers to these and other personal reflective questions are explored in this course on Leadership Empathy Attributes. Numerous techniques, personal examples, empirical case studies, including practice questions at the end of each chapter are used to guide your development and to frame meanings out of the content to improve your acts of empathy leadership process.

ALS II Course 4: Encouragement Leadership Attribute—*The direct measures of encouragement are the inspired strength and quality of uplifted spirit to persevere toward a desired outcome.*

There are times when people want to grow in their potential, want to change their present situation, feel emotionally low in lived experiences, or feel as if they should be appreciated for a job well done. In any of these cases, some encouragement goes a long way to lift up the spirit of someone low. A case study is of the leadership qualities of Barnabas, named the "Son of Encouragement" by the disciples (Acts 4:36), because they saw him as an *encourager*. You can only be an encourager from the strength of your inner personality. The act of encouragement is mostly expressed or *given* to inspire growth or apply a spiritual gift to serve others. What did the disciples see in Barnabas? Obviously, he must have affected them with his acts of encouragement. They saw him as an encourager by his *courage* to *inspire* them at a time they desperately needed to move the ministry forward. This course explores the distinguishing characteristics of encouragement attributes in servant leadership. Each characteristic of encouragement attribute will be discussed in detail with emphasis on strategies of how they can be further developed or practiced by a leader-servant in a leadership process. Practice questions at the end of each chapter are used to guide your development and to frame meanings out of the content to improve your acts of encouragement leadership process.

ALS II Course 5: Initiation Leadership Attribute—*Initiation creates the catalyst for a vision, and the vision when acted upon, produces a desired change.*

The initiation of a process for a desired change is the core of the inner strength of a decisive leader in any leadership process. Initiation leadership is the act of taking step to originate or get something started. In general, initiative is an "individual's action that begins a process, often done without direct managerial influence." The primary outcome of the initiation attribute is that it leads to desired change; something new in the lives of the followers or organization, such as a new growth in followers, a new product or policy in an organization, or a new mission or mission agenda. How do leaders take action to begin a process of change? What are the distinguishing initiation characteristics of leaders such as Moses and Nehemiah in working according to God's agenda? How does a leader conceive a strategic vision for initiation action?. or negotiate his way to influence possible actions toward that vision. This course explores answers to these, and other questions based on examples from Nehemiah (Nehemiah 1:4 through 2:6-8) and Moses and God (Exodus 3 and 4:1-14).

ALS II Course 6: Listening Communication   Leadership Attribute
—*Effective communication occurs at the convergence of listening attention, hearing, and understanding of the information transmitted.*

A leader-servant face three important types of communication at one point or the other. At the core is listening ability as the inner strength and ability to receive and understand the meanings of words and messages internally and accurately in a two-way communication process. How does a leader-servant communication with God, the Holy Spirit, and followers (individually or collectively) to be most effective. The course explores how the three elements—words spoken, unspoken, and in the spirit—offer unique reflections of the communication process and what they share in common. How does listening serve as a critical element of effective communication between people forms the bridge by which a leader can be effective?. A leader's capacity to listen to communicate effectively depends on the leader's inner strength to perceive, hear, and understand the information from written, verbal, and non-verbal exchanges. Each characteristic of listening communications attribute will be discussed in detail with emphasis on strategies of how they can be further developed or practiced by a leader-servant. Practice questions at the end of each chapter are used to guide your development and to frame meanings out of the content to improve your acts of listening leadership process.

ALS II Course 7: Navigation Leadership Attribute—*Leaders who prepare for and chart through a purposeful course of action arrive with their followers at the desired destination.*

The navigation attribute is having a *vision* for the intended destination plus the direction to get there. Having a vision is a quality of the inner strength of a leader and the path that the leader follows in the life journey is often influenced by internal and external factors. The organizational culture and climate collectively combine to make an organization unique through the diversity of employees' characteristics, values, needs, attitudes, and expectations. How does a leader-servant *navigate* and *negotiate* his actions through the organization and people he serves, individually or collectively, to *finish* or *arrive* at his purpose? How do you prepare your followers to *finish* strong or *arrive* at their destinations? This course explores answers to these and other questions and how a leader's inner strength capacity can empower him to navigate the cultural bridges to influence the desired change in others in their personal and professional needs and attitudes.

ALS II Course 8: Responsibility Leadership Attribute—*Leadership responsibility is the measure of the quality of a Leader's accountability for the growth of followers and the organization*

Responsibility leadership refers to possessing the capability and accountability needed in the act of being responsible (trustworthy, dependable, honest, etc.) in a leadership process. At a personal level, it defines the level of your position (pastor, deacon, department head, janitor, etc.) in your church, family, or employment. Responsible leaders in their positions *choose* to emphasize the positive, uplifting, and flourishing side of organizational life. Are there qualities in your position that need to be trained or developed to influence positive outcomes in people and organizations? Organizationally, what are the attributes of the leadership structure, process, and culture that are most conducive for maximizing the growth of followers and organizations in service toward others? How can responsibility qualities be developed to enhance high-quality relationships, emotional competencies, positive communication, beneficial energy development, and positive climates for the effective leader as a servant leadership process? The course explores answers to these and other questions. Distinguishing leadership characteristics of responsibility attributes are identified and discussed in detail. Practice questions at the end of each chapter are used to guide your development and to frame meanings out of the content to improve your acts of responsibility leadership process.

ALS II Course 9: Stewardship Leadership Attribute—*A measure of good stewardship is the entrustments' better and richer growth change at the end than at the beginning*

*Stewardship leadership is the process of u*tilizing and managing the resources entrusted to you by someone. We recognize that God has ownership of everything above, and below the earth. In that context, we are all stewards of what God owns, including our lives but entrusted to us to be managed and maintained in a purposeful manner that will honor God. What are the distinctive servant leadership characteristics of stewardship and how can they be developed? This course explores answers to these questions with reference to servant leadership. Practice questions at the end of each chapter are used to guide your development and to frame meanings out of the content to improve your acts of steward leadership process

ALS II Course 10: Vision Leadership Attribute—*You have a vision when you understand how you get to your mission-purpose and what the future outcome will be relative to your present.*

The vision leadership attribute gives the leader the ability to specify in the present *what* each follower's or group's growth should be in the future, *where* to focus these efforts to meet that growth; *how* he will accomplish all aspects of his mission, *which* future (destination) he aspires to lead the people, and *when* the purpose will be achieved. Leadership without direction leads followers to nowhere. Vision is the most common descriptor of effective leadership and must be clear and inspirational in order to achieve desired purpose. What are the qualities a visionary leader? When was the last time you added brand new challenges to your normal routine to achieve a new you? Answers to these and other questions are explored in this course. The primary characteristics of visionary leadership will be identified and used to frame a principle of leadership vision attribute. Practice questions at the end of each chapter are used to guide your development and to frame meanings out of the content to improve your acts of encouragement leadership process.

Referenced Scriptures

A variety of Bible translations from over 11,200 original Hebrew, Aramaic, and Greek words to about 6,000 English words do exist with variations in meanings and emphases. I am not a biblical scholar and do not pretend to be one; Hence, I have avoided researching the roots of these words and personally prefer New King James Version (NKJV). I have intentionally used other translations for three main reasons; first, to allow for increased impact and alignment of words to the most desired meaning and emphasis in the concepts being addressed. Second, I wanted new and personal discovery of meanings from translations with which I have not been familiar. And third, I wanted to allow readers who may desire translations other than the NKJV the benefit of their preferred translations. Hence, in addition to the NKJV, other translations used in the book include New International Version (NIV), New Living Translation (NLT), King James Version (KJV), English Standard Version (ESV), and Good News Translation (GNT). Unless otherwise specified, NKJV should be assumed.

Sylvanus Nwakanma Wosu

CHAPTER 1
UNDERSTANDING LEADERSHIP ATTRIBUTES

Leadership attribute is the combined acts of two or more distinctive functional leadership characteristics exhibited in service and relationship toward others.

The starting point of our discussion is the understanding of the key functional definitions and concepts that describe the theme of this book. In general, I will define leadership as an integrative process in which a person applies appropriate attributes to guide and influence the sought-after attitudinal changes in others toward accomplishing a particular goal. Specifically, the Leader as Servant Leadership is a process in which a leader intentionally chooses to put the follower's rights and needs above his positional rights and personal needs, and serves, enables, and empowers them for desired spiritual and professional growth that builds thriving communities.

FUNCTIONAL DEFINITIONS

In the context of these definitions, I will begin the descriptions of the leadership attributes of an authentic leader-servant by offering a functional definition of Leadership Attributes, and showing how that definition differs from those of Leadership Character, Characteristics, and Traits.

Leadership Character is the sum total of personal qualities in leadership, such as honesty, values, vision, trust, and so on that make up the moral capital of the leader; Leadership character should describe who the leader is inside or the leader's basic personality traits.

The Leadership Characteristics describe the distinctive characteristics or features of a leader, such as attitudes, competencies, skills, and specific experiences that go beyond his character (personality). Leadership characteristics determine how (through skills and competencies) the leader leads or take actions in the process of leadership in any particular situation;

The Leadership traits are the distinguishing leadership characteristics of a leader (these are things that define his leadership characteristics), which differentiate from personality traits... Leadership traits are the set of characteristics that define a particular leader's leadership. This means that a leadership characteristic is a trait when it is a unique characteristic of the leader.

Leadership Attributes, unlike leadership character, characteristics, and traits, is *a leadership attribute and the combined act of two or more distinctive functional leadership characteristics exhibited in service and relationship toward others* or traits externally displayed in action toward others. All leadership attributes grow out of the leadership inner value system but can be externally displayed predominantly as an outbound or outward attribute or both:

1. **Outbound Attributes:** These are distinctive outward-bound attributes emanating from the inner strength of the leader to support external conduct in service and relationships toward others. They form the internal core functional qualities that motivate or enhance the outward manifestation of the inside character toward others. The outbound attribute such as listening and vision, for example, are the direct results of the inner values of the leader such as patience, hearing, love, humility, or all the fruits of the spirit.

2. **Outward Attributes:** These are distinctive functional outward outer visible attributes emanating from the richness of the outbound and inner values of the leader. For example, external attributes such as Servanthood, emulation/modeling, empathy, etc. are outflows from the leader who will directly impact the follower. Outward attributes can be enriched by the outbound (inner) attributes. As shown in Figure 1, the outward attributes in general form the outer core of

functional attributes in the leader as servant leadership, but they can share some overlapping functions with the outbound attributes.

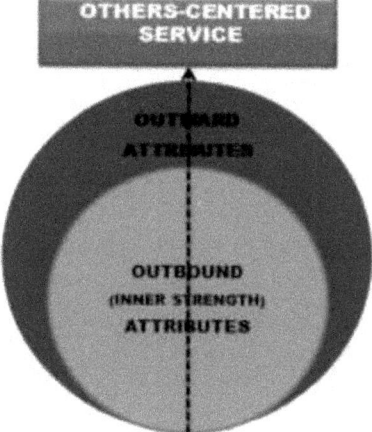

Figure 1.1. Servant leadership functional attributes

In summary, a leadership attribute is more than an ability or a characteristic; it is making those characteristics or abilities functional as part of how the leader acts (his habits) in service to others and applying those characteristics (beyond just having them) in personal and service relations to others. The character or known characteristic defines some aspects of your abilities or who you are inside— e.g. honest, humble, brave, etc. Your attribute, on the other hand, defines your habits; a display of how you use your characteristics, or the actions you exhibit toward others because of who you are inside. For example, empathy as a leadership characteristic becomes a leadership attribute if the followers can distinguish the leader's acts or habits of empathy, such as walking through with his followers in their state of suffering to bring wholeness; otherwise, it is just a characteristic or ability. Leadership attributes toward others are what impact the followers' and the organizational growth more than ability and competence.

In addressing one of the self-righteous hypocritical attributes of servitude leadership, Jesus called leader-servants to be "inside-out" leaders that reflect credibility; indeed, leaders should not appear outwardly righteous when they are full of hypocrisy and lawlessness in their hearts. He was describing "inside–out" as an authentic leadership attribute measured by the display of credibility a leadership attribute!

ALS Initiative Leadership
Attributes, Principles, & Practices

The measuring stick of a leader-servant is Jesus Christ. We measure ourselves unto the measure of the status of the fullness of Christ (Ephesians 4:13).

The leadership attributes of an authentic leader as a servant are encapsulated in **SERVANT/SERVING LEADERSHIP** are listed in Table 1.1, and defined in Table 1.2: *Servanthood, Emulation, Responsibility, Vision, Navigation, Adaptability, Trust, Listening, Empathy, Affection, Discipleship, Encouragement, Reproduction, Stewardship, Healing-Care, Initiation, Integrity,* and *Persuasion*. Other support attributes include *Influence, Courage, and Generosity*.

The attributes have been separated into Outward and Outbound (Inner Strength) leadership Attributes. As shown in Table 1.1, each of these attributes has three or more leadership characteristics. As such, more than 65 leadership characteristics are covered in these 20 attributes. For example, a leader's Servanthood leadership attribute is characterized by his willing servant's heart of selfless role humility, sacrifice, and submissiveness. The more these are present in a leader, the more effective the servant leadership.

Table 1.1: The functional leader-servant leadership Outbound (Inner Strength) and Outward attributes

	LEADER-SERVANT LEADERSHIP ATTRIBUTES			INNER STRENGTH ATTRIBUTES	OUTWARD ATTRIBUTES
S	Servanthood	L	Listening	Adaptability	Affection
E	Emulation	E	Empathy	Courage	Discipleship
R	Responsibility	A	Affection	Empathy	Emulation
V	Vision	D	Discipleship	Encouragement	Generosity
A	Adaptability	E	Encouragement	Initiation	Healing-Care
N	Navigation	R	Reproduction	Listening	Influence
T	Trust	S	Stewardship	Navigation	Persuasion
I	Influence	H	Healing-Care	Responsibility	Reproduction
G	Generosity	I	Initiation	Stewardship	Servanthood
C	Courage	P	Persuasion	Vision	Trust/Integrity

The list does not assume that a leader has to be excellent in all attributes or even have all of them to be an effective Leader–Servant. However, the more of these attributes the leader displays in his acts of service toward others, the more productive he or she will be, and the further his impact on the followers and organization. The table also shows that two or more attributes can share common characteristics, which can be applied or observed in different contexts. For example, a leader's ability to inspire followers can be seen in his acts of discipleship, empowerment, an.d encouragement attributes in the context in which these attributes apply. Each attribute is exhibited either as a part of the outbound inner strength attribute of a leader or a part of the outward attribute. Table 1.1 is not an exhaustive list of attributes; in fact, there are hundreds of such attributes. This is just the starting point.

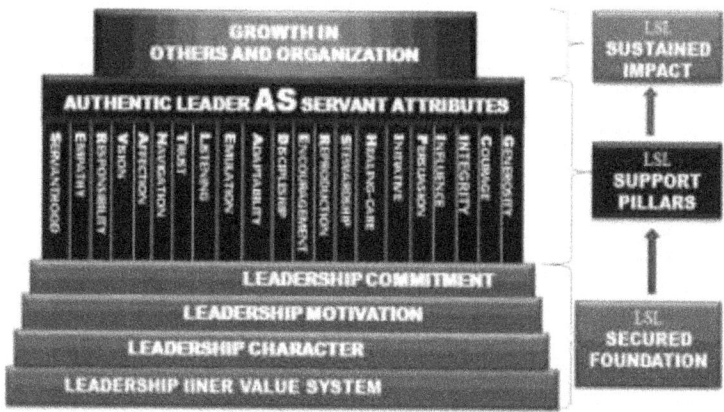

Figure 1.2: Servant leadership outward attributes (dark blue) and relationship to four foundational layers of the LSL Model

Figure 1.2 shows that the leader's attributes are shaped and secured by his four foundational layers (leadership inner value system, leadership character, motivation, and commitment). The attributes of the leader–servants are also conceptualized as the support pillars that will establish and support the personal authenticity of the leader, what the leader, does and the effectiveness of the leadership process. Thus, the attributes represent functional pillars of authentic leadership that can be learned or enriched as described in detail in the subsequent chapters. The combined effect of a secured foundation and stable support pillars will make a sustained impact on the growth of followers and the organization.

COMPARISONS WITH OTHER WORKS

The original works by Greenleaf (1970) in servant leadership [1] have been reviewed by Larry Spears (1996), who identified listening, empathy, healing, awareness, persuasion, conceptualization, foresight, stewardship, commitment to the growth of others, and building community as the ten distinguishing characteristics of servant leadership. [2] Russell (2001) has studied these attributes and have shown them to be essential in servant leadership and concluded that these qualities generally "grow out of the inner values and beliefs of individual leaders." [3] Russell and Stone (2002) extended the Greenleaf 10 attributes to 20 attributes observed in servant-leaders. These 20 attributes were categorized by these authors as either functional attributes (intrinsic characteristics of servant-leaders) or accompanying attributes (complement attributes that enhance the functional attributes).[4] The operational attributes were identified as vision, honesty, integrity, trust, modeling, service, pioneering, appreciation, and empowerment with the accompanying attributes of communication, credibility, competence, stewardship, visibility, influence, persuasion, listening, encouragement, teaching, and delegation. Only three of the attributes identified by Greenleaf were identified, and all three were accompanying attributes rather than functional. Responsibility, adaptability, affection, discipleship, navigation, and reproduction attributes which are considered critical in biblical-based servant leadership in my LSL model are not covered by Russell and Greenleaf. As shown in the description of the attributes in Table 1.2, most of the attributes reported by Russell and Stone (2002)[5] or Greenleaf [1] can be seen either in the twenty attributes or their associated characteristics. Integrity and honesty for example are leadership characteristics of trust and other attributes rather than an independent attributes. I take the position that servant leadership attributes are functional attributes in acts of duty to others and emanate from the inner value system of the leader.

CHAPTER 1
UNDERSTANDING LEADERSHIP ATTRIBUTES

Table 1.2: Description of the functional leader-servant outward leadership attributes and associated principles and characteristics

Leader–Servant Leadership Attributes	Principles of Leadership Attributes	Leadership Characteristics
Affection: *This is the combined love-based works toward providing the essential help or services for the spiritual growth or survival of another person. .* (Chapter 2)	*Affection flows from a person to produce positive emotions for the well-being of another person*	Kindness Compassion Practical Love Affective signs Appreciation
Discipleship: *This is the combined acts of personally developing, intentionally equipping, and attentively empowering growth in others to reproduce a heart of service.* (Chapter 3)	*Discipleship transforms and empowers followers for service leadership that grows communities.*	Inspiring Shepherding Equipping Developing Empowering
Emulation: *This is the combined acts of initiating an authentic servant attitude as a model of service worthy of following* (Chapter 4)	*A great leader-servant outwardly and positively inspires a pattern of good works for others to follow.*	Inspiration Motivation Initiation Model Following
Generosity: *This is the combined acts of freely sharing with and giving to others as an act of kindness, without expectation of reward or return to him.* (Chapter 5)	*Generosity is an outward measure of the level of sacrifice, what is shared, or the impact a giving makes, not just the size of the giving.*	Sharing Giving Kindness Affection Love
Healing-Care: *This is the combined acts of providing comfort and empathy to make others whole emotionally and spiritually along with tending to the follower's physical and mental well-being.* (Chapter 6)	*Comforting others in any trouble with the comfort with which we are comforted by God, brings healing - wholeness.*	Self-Healing Empathy Reconciliation Comfort Relational
Influence: *This is the combined acts of positively affecting desired change in conduct,*	*The true measure of leadership success in affecting*	Model Positive attitude Authority

41

performance, and relational connections toward others-centered course of action or service. (Chapter 7)	desired change in conduct, performance, and relational connections in others is influence	Connection Wisdom Intelligence,
Persuasion: This is the combined acts of communicating perspective to connect, challenge, and convince with a compelling purpose to convert others to a new position. (Chapter 8)	The means of transforming others to a new perspective is through empathetic persuasion	Connecting Challenging Communicating Convincing Converting Encouraging
Reproduction: This is the combined acts of developing your leadership qualities in others and releasing them as successors to continue a greater mission. (Chapter 9)	Great leaders produce successors for legacy and greater courses as an expected product of an effective leadership reproduction.	Selecting Mentoring Equipping Empowering Releasing
Servanthood: This is the combined acts of humility, willingness, and intentionality in service to others through selfless sacrifice and submission as a servant. (Chapter 10)	A leader-servant is most qualified to lead when most ready to serve as a servant for the growth of others. The role of a leader is to serve as a servant	Servant's heart Humility Sacrifice Service Willingness Submissiveness
Trust: This is the combined acts of positive display of character, competence, credibility, and shared relational connections that produce assured trust-confidence of the trustee in the trusted. (Chapter 11)	True leadership trust produces assured trustee's confidence and readiness to follow based on the credibility, competence, and shared relational connections of the trusted.	Character Competence Integrity Credibility Confidence

PRINCIPLE OF LEADERSHIP ATTRIBUTE

In the context of servant leadership, a leadership attribute is a level above the leadership characteristic or trait of a leader. The principle of leadership attribute states that every leadership attribute has a set of distinguishing characteristics that make up the inward or outward display of the attribute. The principle reflects the essential designed purpose or outcome of the attribute or the inevitable consequence of the effective practice of the attribute. Thus, the principle of leadership attribute is a concise statement about the fundamental truth, value, or belief about the attribute in a leadership situation; it is a statement that establishes an idea about the outcome of the attribute for guiding the practical application of the attribute and its characteristics. I will postulate and frame each principle as an additive function of the characteristics of the attribute. A statement of each principle is quoted at the beginning or below the title of each chapter. It is yet to be experimentally proven if the attribute is a linear or some other non-linear function of these characteristics as variables. It is expected, however, that each character will contribute to the effectiveness of the attribute in varying degrees.

AUTHENTIC LEADERSHIP ATTRIBUTES

At a personal level, attributes are the value-based inside-out moral leadership assets that can be related to the authenticity of a leader-servant. The complexity of defining authenticity has been noted in the literature. The subject of authentic leadership is well covered in the works of Terry (1993),[5] George (2003),[6] and Shair and Eilam (2005).[7] All appear to agree that authenticity requires self-awareness and objective self-identity in personal and social interactions with others. In his book, *Advocacy Leadership*, Professor Gary L. Anderson offers individual, organizational, and societal perspectives on authenticity: "Authenticity, at a peculiar level, is living a life, whether in the private or professional term. This is congruent with one's espoused values; at the structural level, authenticity has to do with viewing human beings as ends in themselves, rather than means to other ends; at the public level, it is a state of affairs that is congruous with the shared political and cultural values of society."[8]

The basic tenets of these perspectives are very fitting to authenticity as a qualifying element of leader-servant leadership attributes. The attribute reflects how the followers see the leader based on the leader's distinctive features displayed through his or her actions personally, organizationally, and societally. The leader is seen as a leader-servant or serving leader because the followers see him lead as a servant from an inside-out value of others. This is what makes the leader authentic.

Authenticity means that what a leader displays outside, in personal or leadership life of service to others, and society is based on the values the leader espouses inside.

Authenticity in servant leadership can be one or two types or both: *Outbound Authenticity and Outward Authenticity*: The Outbound (outward-bound) Authenticity is the genuineness of personal honesty from your inner strength and abilities; what you say and how you act emanate from who you are or how you feel inside. It reflects the essential truth and honesty about your outward-bound inner strength.

Outward authenticity, on the other hand, describes the truthfulness of your credibility and honesty displayed outward in relation to others; your *outer* visible behavior or how you act outwardly towards others reflects exactly your true intentions.

While *outward* authenticity is the visible *outer* indicator of the truth of who you are inside, *outbound* authenticity is outward-bound attribute from the inside of who you are. Credibility in this context is the influence a leader has to attract believability, trustworthiness, and authenticity; it is the believability, trustworthiness, and authenticity of who you are inside and outside.

A key element of personal authenticity is that it is seen or measured in the context of societal, cultural, and organizational interactions. In that context, achieving individual authenticity becomes a challenge since it is influenced by social factors and dispositions of individuals who usually depend on liberal and organizational realities. However, for leader-servant leadership, the leader can face those changing times by remaining focused on his key Biblical-based principles or *Leadership Inner Value System*. Thus, I am interested in authenticity as an essential element of effective Leader-servant leadership attributes or Leader-servant leadership attributes as drivers of leadership authenticity. With that in mind, the first critical element of authenticity in practicing or developing efficient leader-servant leadership attributes is inside-out self-examination relative to the people served rather than the organization. You may ask yourself: What will be my response when the people I lead act or react in a certain way, will it be negative or positive? What are my strengths and vulnerabilities at those times?

Professor Yacobi in his post, "Elements of Human Authenticity," noted that since "the self -arise attribute emerges from interactions between self, others, and the environment in a complex society and world, there may co-exist multiple complicated identities depending on place and context." [9] He went on to identify the following <u>essential elements of personal authenticity</u>: self-awareness, unbiased self-examination, accurate self-knowledge, reflective judgment, personal responsibility, and integrity, genuineness, and humility, empathy for others, understanding of others, optimal utilization of feedback from others. All of these are covered under the leadership attributes or characteristics shown in Table 1.2.

Bill George, in his book, *Authentic Leadership*, takes the position that to be an authentic leader; a person must have the following essential characteristics: [10]

- Behavior based on value: He must understand his own values and exhibit behavior to others based on those values;
- He must not compromise his values in difficult situations but could use the situation to strengthen personal values in those situations.
- Passion from a clear purpose: Be self-aware of who he is, where he is going, and the right thing to do.
- Compassion from the heart: He must lead from a compassionate heart that allows them to be sensitive to the plight and needs of others,
- Connectedness from a relationship; he must be relationally connected with people he leads,
- Consistency from the self-disciple: He must demonstrate self-discipline to remain calm, collected, and consistent in a stressful situation.

Modeled after the elements above, Table 1.3 lists six essential characteristics of authenticity for servant leadership. These fundamental characteristics cover the five identified above and can also be aligned with the leadership characteristics in Table 1.2. Each attribute in Table 1.2 is expected to pass the personal authenticity test in Tables 1.3, 1.4. In a survey of 132 Christian leaders, seventy-four percent (74%) of them agreed that they always or frequently exhibit servant leadership attributes. [11] Thus, a pass of the outward authenticity test means that a pure leader must demonstrate 70% or more of these essential elements of this legitimacy. (That is, 70% YES in the assessment questions in Tables 1.3, 1.4).

It needs to be noted, however, that a secular leader could be authentic and still lack some of the essential servant leadership attributes or characteristics such as selflessness, servanthood, and love-motivated servant attitudes of a leader-servant. Effective leader-servants are authentic leaders and personal authenticity is an essential element of leader-servant leadership. The key test for leader-servant authenticity is the quality of his inside-out value and personal character. What is most important is a change from the inside-out.

Table 1.3: The test of essential elements of personal inner strength authenticity in servant leadership

	Elements of Inner Strength Authenticity	Inner Strength (Outbound) Authenticity Assessment Questions	YES / NO
1	Personal inside-out value-based behavior	Are your personal inside-out values aligned with acts of service and behavior outside?	1
		Are you honest to yourself in relation to your inner strengths and abilities?	2
2	Inside-out Self-Awareness	Do you have unbiased self-examination, and accurate self-knowledge of who you are inside-out?	3
		Do you know your inner strength and weaknesses in relation to the good you want to show as an outward attribute?	4
3	Inside-out Empathy-Compassion	Do you know and feel from your inside what you want for your followers?	5
		Are you motivated to empathize, based on your inside feelings?	6
4	Inside-out Connection with followers	Do you feel deep, personal, and spiritual connection with your followers?	7
		Does what you say and how you act reflect how you feel when you relate to others?	8
5	Inside-out Emotional Self-regulation	Do you have difficulty controlling your emotion in order to remain calm in a stressful situation?	9
		Are you always able to comfort yourself?	10
6	Inside-out Authenticity Feedback	Do your followers see your inside-out value from your outside behavior?	11
		Will your followers feel that what you say you are is congruent with how you act?	12
#YESs_____ ; # NOs_____ : Outbound Authenticity: YES/ 12-----%			

CHAPTER 1
UNDERSTANDING LEADERSHIP ATTRIBUTES

Table 1.4: The test of essential elements of personal outward authenticity in servant leadership

	Elements of Personal Outward Authenticity	Personal Outward Authenticity Assessment Questions	YES or NO
1	Personal value-based outward behavior	Are your personal values and beliefs aligned with your acts of service and behavior toward others?	1
		Do you live out your life according to your beliefs?	2
2	Personal Self-Awareness	Do you have clarity of your personal vision and purpose?	3
		Does what you know about yourself accurately describe what others say?	4
3	Personal Outward Empathy-Compassion	Do you apply how you feel to what your followers need?	5
		Do you lead from a compassionate heart and are you sensitive to the plight and needs of others?	6
4	Personal Connection with followers	Do you feel deep, personal connection with your followers?	7
		Does your outward action toward others reflect exactly your true intentions?	8
5	Outward Emotional Self-regulation	Do you have difficulty controlling your emotions to remain calm in a stressful situation?	9
		Does your evaluation of your value of others agree with how valued they feel?	10
6	Personal Authenticity Feedback	Do your followers see your outward acts as true and honest?	11
		Can your followers see other-centeredness in 70% or more of your attributes?	12
#YESs_____ ; # NOs_____: Outbound Authenticity: YES/ 12-----%			

ALS INITIATIVE LEADERSHIP
ATTRIBUTES, PRINCIPLES, & PRACTICES

SUMMARY 1
UNDERSTANDING LEADERSHIP PROCESS

Before starting this exercise, please read and follow the instruction in the preface of this workbook. Answers to these questions are contained in this chapter. Completion of these exercises after reading the chapter should take 60-90 minutes.

Discovering the Leadership Attributes

1. What is your alternative definition of leadership? In learning to lead, how would you differentiate the following elements:
    a. Leadership.
    b. Leader as servant leadership.
    c. Leadership characteristics.
    d. Leadership attributes.
2. What are the key differences between the Leader as Servant and the Servant as Leader Leadership philosophies?
3. What was the original source of the Servant as Leader (SL)? What was the original source of Leader as Servant (LS)?
4. What is the key framework of a Leader as a Servant Leadership?
5. Authenticity in servant leadership can be one or two types or both *Outbound Authenticity and Outward Authenticity*. Describe a time when you displayed:
    a. The Outbound (outward-bound)—*outbound* authenticity is outward-bound attribute from the inside of who you are.
    b. *The Outward Authenticity—outward* authenticity is the visible *outer* indicator of the truth of who you are inside,
6. Describe the key elements of personal authenticity seen or measured in the context of societal, cultural, and organizational interactions.
7. How are the essential characteristics of authentic leader in leadership process in challenging times?
8. How much of a leader-servant are you? Take the personal leader-servant audit in Table 1.5 to self-assess your effectiveness.
9. Based on the questions in Table 1.5, can you identify each of the twenty attributes? What ones did you score 3 ("sometimes") or less than 3? Review and learn and commit to work to improve.

CHAPTER 1
UNDERSTANDING LEADERSHIP ATTRIBUTES

Table 1.5. Leader As Servant-Leadership Audit

A servant-leader in his leadership position purposefully choses to serve and inspire acts of service in others by his example. Select and circle best answer to questions
1=Never: 2=Almost never ; 3=Sometimes; 4=Frequently; 5 =Always

	Servant Leadership assessment questions	Circle no				
1	I am willing and other-centered, and readily chose to serve others as a servant for their personal growth	1	2	3	4	5
2	I model others-centered attitude in my service and relationships and inspire same for others to follow	1	2	3	4	5
3	I have a sense of obligation, willingness, and accountability for the service towards others	1	2	3	4	5
4	I have the foresightedness to specify in the present view what others' growth should be in a given future	1	2	3	4	5
5	I work toward providing the essential help or services for the spiritual growth or survival of the others;	1	2	3	4	5
6	I provide the needed purposeful course of action for how to chart the course to for my followers.	1	2	3	4	5
7	I display external credibility and a strong sense of character based on values, beliefs, and competence;	1	2	3	4	5
8	In communication, I attentively perceive and hear what is communicated, reflectively listen to understand and to be understood	1	2	3	4	5
9	I walk through with others in their state (suffering, emotions, etc.) in a way that provides the needed care and well-being	1	2	3	4	5
10	I have a measure of self-secured flexibility to adapt appropriate attitude to serve all people in different situations	1	2	3	4	5
11	I personally develop, intentionally equip, and attentively nurture spiritually growth in others	1	2	3	4	5
12	My act of bravery instills in others the courage and confidence to follow or persevere in a course of action	1	2	3	4	5
13	I develop my leadership qualities in others as successors to continue in a purposeful mission	1	2	3	4	5
14	I manage , maintain,, and account for all resources entrusted to me and being responsible for the difference my acts make	1	2	3	4	5
15	As a care-giver, I act to comfort and make others whole emotionally	1	2	3	4	5
16	When I see a need, I originate a vision and action, and stay committed to meet that need and desired change	1	2	3	4	5

ALS INITIATIVE LEADERSHIP
ATTRIBUTES, PRINCIPLES, & PRACTICES

17	I display a holistic view of an issue to inform, transform or convert others to my view through empathetic persuasion	1	2	3	4	5
18	I freely share what I have sacrificially as an act of kindness to others, without expectation of reward in return	1	2	3	4	5
19	My act of influence is to affect the actions, behavior, opinions, etc., of others based on trust, credibility and relationship	1	2	3	4	5
20	In the face challenges and danger, I act with bravery to overcome fear and take a stand with strength and conviction	1	2	3	4	5
Score Range	Add up the numbers in each column (Total Score____ Check and Understand the key areas to work on					
81-100	Strong Leader-Servant; keep it up, go and train others.					
66-80	Above average Leader-Servant; work 25% of key areas					
50-65	Average but developing; need to work on 50% of key areas					
34-49	Below average leader; work on 75% of key areas					
<34	Not a Leader-Servant; need training in all areas					

CHAPTER 2
INITIATION LEADERSHIP ATTRIBUTE

Initiation creates the catalyst for a vision, and the vision when acted upon, produces a desired change.

The initiation of a process for a desired change is the core of the inner strength of a decisive leader in any leadership process.
Initiation is the act of taking step to originate or get something started. In general, initiative is an "individual's action that begins a process, often done without direct managerial influence." [12]. How do leaders take action to begin a process of change? When man sinned against God, how did God initiate the process of change to reconcile man to Him? What are the distinguishing initiation characteristics of leaders such as Moses and Nehemiah in working according to God's agenda? Answers to these and other questions are explored in this chapter based on examples from Nehemiah (Nehemiah 1:4 through 2:6-8) and Moses and God (Exodus 3 and 4:1-14).

SERVANT LEADERSHIP INITIATIVE ATTRIBUTE

The initiation attribute affords a leader the inner instinctive ability to conceive a vision or commitment to lead the process of the desired change. The first characteristic that can be observed externally is a *commitment* to a strategic *vision*. The vision may be the leaders, like in the case of Nehemiah, to rebuild the broken gates or may have been instilled by someone else, as in the case of Moses, who was to carry out God's vision and agenda to bring the Children of Israel out of Egypt. Visionary leaders are good initiators; they see farther than others can see, and they are passionate to initiate action based on their convictions. Once the strategic vision has been conceived or committed to, the leader must negotiate or *influence* possible actions toward that vision. The negotiation may require positively influencing people toward buy-in. Vision and influence are the starting point to begin the process but not enough to complete the process; the leader must *focus* on the essential priorities with the end in mind.

PRINCIPLE OF LEADERSHIP INITIATIVE ATTRIBUTE

Initiation is the act of taking initiative in something—in leadership, education, service, etc. The primary outcome of the initiation attribute is that it leads to desired change; something new in the lives of the followers or organization, such as a new growth in followers, a new product or policy in an organization, or a new mission or mission agenda. Hardly can anything happen without someone originating it, usually as a personal inner drive or vision, and acting or influencing needed action to see that come through In general, the initiative is an "individual's action that begins a process, often done without direct managerial influence." [42]. Based on these characteristics, a functional definition is as follows:

> *Servant leadership initiation attribute is the combined acts of originating a vision influence, focus, and action toward a desired change.*

Influence as a characteristic of initiation requires a leader's ability to inspire others to join in the action to initiate the process without any external coercion on the leader or the initiator. Initiation is a four-stage model that most ends in action. This additive process leads me to the principle below:

> *Servant leadership initiation principle: Initiation creates the catalyst for a vision, and the vision when acted upon, produces a desired change.*

This can be expressed as:

VISION + INFLUENCE + FOCUS + ACTION = INITIATION

Figure 6 shows a four-stage initiation process model that starts with a vision–initiation and ends at action–initiation. Each stage of initiation builds on the preceding stage toward a desired outcome.

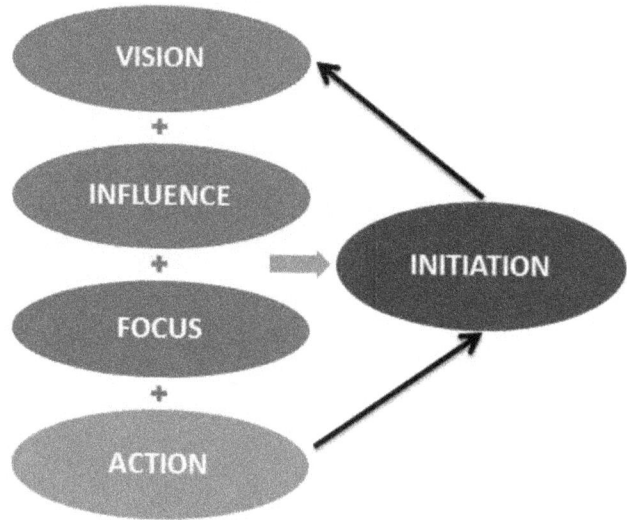

Figure 6: Four-stage process model of servant leadership initiation attribute

SUMMARY 2
INITIATIVE LEADERSHIP ATTRIBUTE

Before starting this exercise, please read and follow the instruction in the preface of this workbook. Answers to these questions are contained in this chapter. Completion of these exercises after reading the chapter should take 60-90 minutes.

Discovering Initiative Leadership Attributes

1. What are the distinguishing initiation characteristics of leaders such as Moses and Nehemiah in working according to God's agenda?
2. Give a functional definition Servant leadership initiation attribute

ALS Initiative Leadership Attributes, Principles, & Practices

3. What are some example of initiative leadership in the bible (from Nehemiah (Nehemiah 1:4 through 2:6-8) and Moses and God (Exodus 3 and 4:1-14).
4. What is the role of initiation attribute in leadership?

Understanding the Principle of Leadership Initiative Attribute

1. Initiation is the act of taking step to originate or get something started. What is the primary outcome of the initiation attribute?
2. What does Influence as a characteristic of initiation require in a leader?
3. What is the additive law or process of initiative leadership attribute?

Practicing Initiation leadership Attribute

1. What would you consider the key characteristics of the initiation leadership attribute?
2. How many acts of the initiation as an attribute do you display? Take the leadership initiation Attribute, audit in Table 5.1
3. Based on the statements in Table AII.5, can you identify each of the characteristic? What ones did you score 3 ("sometimes") or less than 3?
4. With reference to initiation leadership attribute, what take-away, meaning or lesson can you frame to improve your acts of initiation in a leadership process?
5. Write a personal commitment how to improve

CHAPTER 2
INITIATIVE LEADERSHIP ATTRIBUTE

	Table AII.5 . Initiation-Attribute Audit: Servant leadership initiation-attribute is the *combined acts of originating a vision influence, focus, and action toward a desired change.* Assess the quality of leadership initiation-attribute by inserting an X under the number that best describes your response to each item statement.					
	Initiation-Attribute Check 1= Always; 2= Frequently; 3= Sometimes; 4= Almost Never; 5= Never	1	2	3	4	5
1	I originate actions based on my understanding of what matters most to the followers or organization					
2	I initiate servant ministry in others					
3	I encourage followers in order to receive buy-in through persuasion:					
4	I have the foresightedness for correct perspective					
5	I am able to see a need and possible solution in my acts of initiation					
6	I align my commitment for change to action for the desired change.					
7	I am usually able to inspire the actions for the initiation process for change.					
6	I am spiritually focused to know enough to act					
8	I know where the follower or organization is going in my leading					
9	I am not afraid to take risk-but plans ahead for any mistake					
10	I have the gut instincts-with vision- passion to act in most situations					
	Add up you're rating in each column					
Score Rage	Guide and Explanation of Score: understand the areas you need to develop	Total Score =				
10-17:	Great Initiator, keep it up!					
18-25:	Above Average- Initiator; need to work on 25% of the areas					
26-33:	Average Initiator; need to work on 50% of the areas					
34-41:	Below average, need to work on 75% of the areas					
42-50:	Not an Initiator; work all areas					

CHAPTER 3
DEVELOPING INITIATION-VISION

The initiation-vision stage is the vision-originating driver of the actions that begin the process of initiation for desired change. It is characterized by the leader's ability to see and evaluate the future, good or bad, from the present. It is having the courage and foresight to know when and why to act without being told.

An initiation vision defines the *initiation–purpose*; that is, the *reason* for the initiation, the initiation direction of *how and where* to begin, and the *initiation-courage* to start the initiation process. Nehemiah as a leader saw how Jerusalem laid waste with its gates burned down as a reproach in the future for the people. "Then I said to them, "You see the distress that we are in, how Jerusalem lays waste, and its gates are burned with fire. Nehemiah's example showed a leader who knew *where* he was going in his vision, *how* long the project would last, *how* to get to his desired goal, *who* to trust in the work, and *what* he must have to get the project done. He also needed to know what the people wanted and desired to see the wall rebuilt. "Come and let us build the wall of Jerusalem, that we may no longer be a reproach" (Nehemiah 2:17). Here in this Scripture you see a leader with a vision-purpose and courage to start the rebuilding process. His foresightedness comes from the inner strength that inspires him to see what others were not seeing.

Moses followed God's agenda to free the Jews because of the slavery conditions he saw and experienced, and God's vision originated the process for their freedom. God had to make Moses learn and submit to be able to implement His plan. We can develop a vision–initiation by the following:

FORESIGHTED WITH THE CORRECT PERSPECTIVE

Initiation-vision is the foresightedness for correct perspective or the leader's ability to see a need and possible solution before and farther than others can see. Initiation is usually taken to influence a desired change that has been foresighted. The success of such an initiative depends on the ability to clearly map out the destination from the present location. The vision–initiation is effective to the extent that the leader can conceive what is needed in the entire initiation process.

The Bible says,

> *"Sing, O barren, You who have not borne! Break forth into singing, and cry aloud, You who have not labored with child!...Enlarge the place of your tent, And let them stretch out the curtains of your dwellings; Do not spare; Lengthen your cords, And strengthen your stakes. For you shall expand to the right and to the left...Do not fear, for you will not be ashamed...And will not remember the reproach of your widowhood anymore" (Isaiah 54:1-4 NKJV).*

This is prophetic Scripture of God's promised comfort and peace for His people. The end and the desired change envisioned are covenants for future joy and peace, from a state of barrenness. God is calling "the barren" to rejoice and be prepared for an increase that will spread and expand all around and beyond their expectations. The initiative to enlarge your place or accomplish a sought-after goal and expectations; must have a perspective that has that goal in view. Thus, your vision–perspective for the desired goal is determined by the limitations of your mind or what you can conceive from what you see. Such a perspective creates the correct vision–initiation. The vision initiation is also what begins the process of initiation. This requires having the correct vision-driven attitudes such as the courage to act, commitment to the desired change, motivation to follow the process, and foresightedness to see the change as desirable, both for the leader and the followers. The initiation-vision attitude aligns commitment to the initiation with the need for action to make the desired change.

CHAPTER 3
DEVELOPING INITIATION-VISION

BEING COURAGEOUS TO INITIATE

The catalyst that starts the vision–initiation process is initiation-courage. The primary impediment to people taking initiative is fear of the unknown or fear of resistance from people for change. Courage and faith are the antidotes to such fear. Good initiators are usually those who are able to fight and triumph over their fears; they are those who are best at taking risks and can see farther than what others can see.

A critical vision–initiation attitude to build the courage to overcome fear is prayer and faith and walking with God, for only God clearly sees the future. Jesus spent a lot of time with the Father for every initiative step He took in His ministry. Although Jesus is God, he considered time with His Father a critical beginning element for any action. We saw this, too, in Moses and Joshua, who always sought the Lord before any major initiative step. Before his initiative to start the rebuilding process, Nehemiah spent time in prayer. We learn from the walks of these leaders with God that prayer helps the leader build courage, assume the burden, and deepen his conviction in the action. Indeed, prayer focuses on the leader's vision to see more clearly what God's agenda is in the desired change. Prayer stills a leader's heart and allows him to wait to receive or hear from God; prayer serves as a source of encouragement and power for the leader; and prayer initiates the fulfillment of the vision by increasing the leader's confidence and dependence on God to act (Nehemiah 1:1-11). Nehemiah displayed a positive attitude, value, courage, and commitment to the process as a way of influencing the people to follow without fear. Servant leadership is serving by leading followers toward the desired change.

ALS INITIATIVE LEADERSHIP
ATTRIBUTES, PRINCIPLES, & PRACTICES

SUMMARY 3
DEVELOPING INITIATION-VISION

Before starting this exercise, please read and follow the instruction in the preface of this workbook. Answers to these questions are contained in this chapter. Completion of these exercises after reading the chapter should take 60-90 minutes.

Discovering the Acts of Initiation-Vision

1. Define initiation-vision. How can initiation-vision stage be characterized?
2. Define the initiation-*purpose* and initiative-*courage*. How did prophet Nehemiah as a leader demonstrate theses (Nehemiah 2:17)?
3. What does the Bible teach about initiation-vision (Isaiah 54:1-4 NKJV)?
4. How does initiation-vision attitude align commitment to the initiation with the need for action to make the desired change?

Practicing the Acts of Initiative-Vision

1. **Initiation-Vision** is the foresightedness for correct perspective or a leader's ability to see a need and possible solution before and farther than others can see.
   a. What is required in a leader to have effective vision initiation?
   b. How vision–initiation attitude aligns commitment to the need for action to make the desired change?
   c. In what ways did Moses demonstrate vision–initiation as the foresightedness for correct perspective or the leader's ability to see a need and possible solution before and farther than others can see?
2. How is being Courageous to Initiate as an act of initiation -vision the catalyst that starts the vision–initiation?
3. How is prayer with faith the critical vision–initiation attitude to build the courage to overcome fear?
4. Prayer initiates the fulfillment of the vision by increasing the leader's confidence and dependence on God to act.

Chapter 3
Developing Initiation-Vision

    a. How did Nehemiah display a positive attitude, value, courage, and commitment to the process as a way of influencing the people to follow without fear (Nehemiah 1:1-11).)?
5. With reference to initiation leadership attribute, what take-away, meaning or lesson can you frame to improve your acts of initiation-vision in a leadership process?
6. Write a personal commitment how to improve.

CHAPTER 4
DEVELOPING INITIATION-INFLUENCE

The Initiation-influence stage is where the leader influences others to join in an action to initiate the process of change. It is an inspiration stage for the actions in the initiation process. This can be developed through the following influence–actions:

INFLUENCE BUY-IN FOR ACTION BY INSPIRATION

To inspire the needed actions for initiation which will involve the people; Nehemiah's example and his success that followed showed that leaders must positively influence people to buy into an initiation process. His method included casting the vision to build the needed synergy for rebuilding and encouraging followers. He explained to them the reason for the desired change; indeed, the individual and collective benefits of rebuilding were explained to them before asking them what was required. He let the followers see the reasons and expressed his comments on the vision–mission. In the end, the people saw joining in the rebuilding process as the only option and did not mind the challenges and risks to their lives.

INFLUENCE BY DECISIVE CONVICTION

Leaders influence others to follow by acts of decisiveness and passionate conviction. The direct result of influence is people's willingness to join in the action. Such willingness can be cultivated in the people by the leaders showing self-will and self-determination. There is no room for indecision if others are to see the worth of the initiative. The leader must be able to push and influence followers to join in the action by first building a consensus based on facts and his conviction. He must be decisive on what is needed and not afraid to act but also plans for any mistakes. Initiation attribute requires a leader-servant to go with his gut instincts-with vision- passion.

INFLUENCE BY AN OUTWARD COMMITMENT

Leaders lead others to commit to a mission through their outward commitment and self-confidence. A leader's commitment and self-confidence in the success of the initiation process must be externally displayed for followers to see and be inspired. Followers must see the leader leading by showing his commitment to the mission. The initiative that carries more people along cannot be led from behind but must be led from the front. When Moses finally took the charge to lead the Children of Israel out of Egypt, he was always at the front of the line. This was also the case with Nehemiah. He motivated his followers toward the vision, by letting them see the reason for their distress: Jerusalem lay at waste and the situation was a reproach to Israel; with the ruined wall, no one was protected. He encouraged followers by building their confidence and assuring them that God's hand was on him and had given him a favor. Even the King had given him permission to come and rebuild. The leaders God used to initiate important actions in history—Moses, Joshua, Nehemiah, Apostle Paul, and others—all displayed incredible commitment and self-confidence in their leadership walk, and the followers were motivated to join in the mission by their commitments.

SUMMARY 4
DEVELOPING INITIATION-INFLUENCE

Before starting this exercise, please read and follow the instruction in the preface of this workbook. Answers to these questions are contained in this chapter. Completion of these exercises after reading the chapter should take 60-90 minutes.

Discovering the Acts of Initiation-Influence
1. What happens at the Initiation-influence stage?
2. Why is this stage described as the inspiration stage for the action?

CHAPTER 4
DEVELOPING INITIATION-INFLUENCE

Practicing the Acts of Initiation-Influence

1. **Initiation-Influence** is a stage that inspires the actions for the initiation process for change.
    a. List your three influence actions for initiation of a desired outcome
    b. How can this be accomplished?
    c. How did Prophet Nehemiah practice the following acts?
    d. Influence Buy-In For Action by Inspiration?
        i. Influence by Decisive Conviction
        ii. Influence by an Outward Commitment
2. With reference to initiation leadership attribute, what take-away, meaning or lesson can you frame to improve your acts of initiation-influence in a leadership process?
3. Write a personal commitment how to improve.

CHAPTER 5
DEVELOPING INITIATION-FOCUS

After initiating the vision, influencing and inspiring people to see the vision as you see it, you must identify the possible actions to focus on and decide which action is most likely to lead to the initiation. The initiation-focus is the visual focus stage that prioritizes actions for the initiation of the process for change through the following focus-actions:

FOCUS ON YOUR VISION-PURPOSE

0A vision to initiate a purpose means nothing unless it is clear and the leader is able to focus on the priorities to accomplish the purpose. By the example of Jesus and others like Paul, we can learn and walk in their steps. Jesus ran His own race by enduring all hardships and fixing His eyes on the final eternal purpose. From Apostle Paul's ministry, we learned that to be focused on our vision-purpose, we watch for pitfalls aside from every encumbrance (burden, load, and hindrances) that will try to prevent us from reaching our goals.

FOCUS WITH A PASSION TO COMPLETE THE PROCESS

Initialization leads to a desired change only when the initiated process is complete. We must not expend our time on goals we cannot complete. This means that we must focus on completing the process. We must run with every step that brings us closer to completing the agenda. This means that we must run with a champion attitude and in such a way as to win whatever the highest prize, no matter the challenges. It means aiming beyond the mountain top, toward the sky above it, so that if we miss the sky, we land at the mountain top; if we miss the Gold, we can still win the Silver. However, If you aim at the mountain top and drive yourself to that limit, and miss it, you will land at the valley. The altitude you reach in your vertical journey for good success is only limited by your passion and winning attitude. Passion gives us the inspiration and motivation to stay focused to complete the race (serving, caring, building, mentoring, healing, etc.). You must have the courage to confront the truth by taking an honest inventory of your life, your talent, your education, and your competencies in relation to the specifics of the initiative for the desired change. An attitude that does not drive you toward initiating a priority action toward your goal will never afford you the needed passion to complete the goal; instead, it may kill your motivation and passion.

FOCUS SPIRITUALLY TO ACT ON THE INITIATION

There is the need to be spiritually focused to know enough to act. This does not mean that you need to know 100% of the information you need to act. In fact, you may never have all the required information. However, you need to have enough of the essential information to initiate the process for the desired change; the goal is for the initiation process to culminate in action.

SUMMARY 5
DEVELOPING THE INITIATION-FOCUS

Before starting this exercise, please read and follow the instruction in the preface of this workbook. Answers to these questions are contained in this chapter. Completion of these exercises after reading the chapter should take 60-90 minutes.

Discovering the Acts of Initiation focus
1. Define initiation-focus.
2. What is the role of initiation-focus stage after vision?

CHAPTER 5
DEVELOPING INITIATION-FOCUS

Practicing the Acts of Initiation-Focus

1. **Initiation-focus** provides the priority actions for the initiation of a process for change.
    a. What are some focus actions you can take?
    b. .How initiation focus serve as visual focus stage that prioritizes actions for the initiation of the process?
2. How can we practice following focus–actions?:
    a. Focus on Your Vision–Purpose
    b. Focus with a passion to complete the process
    c. (Focus spiritually to act on the initiation
3. What does passion give in order to stay focused to complete the race?
4. With reference to initiation leadership attribute, what take-away, meaning or lesson can you frame to improve your acts of initiation-focus in a leadership process?
5. Write a personal commitment how to improve.

CHAPTER 6
DEVELOPING INITIATION-ACTION

Initiation-action is the final implementation stage of the initiation process. It defines the action plan that fuses the other three stages for the concluding process. Without action, vision, influence, and focus all will be abandoned and lost, and the desired change will not occur. A few initiations–action strategies include:

A CASE OF INITIATING A PROCESS OF CHANGE

Why do leaders often give reasons for inaction to initiate a process of change? Sometimes it is procrastination, or an unwillingness to act. How do we understand when excuses are no longer an option for inaction? The case of Moses, a servant of God, illustrates his struggles to understand the how, what, when, and why of the desired change God was calling him to initiate. God had called Moses to join him in initiating the action to free the Children of Israel, who were oppressed in Egypt. God wanted to deliver them, and He wanted Moses to join with Him to initiate the process for their deliverance (Exodus 3:7-10). God wanted to fulfill His purpose and was calling Moses to His desired purpose to initiate a series of actions. First, Moses had to go to Pharaoh and tell him to let God's people go. Second, Moses had to lead God's people out of Egypt through His power and guidance into the land He promised their forefathers. But Moses saw himself differently than God's perspective and gave the following five excuses why he was not the one to initiate that process:

1. **Who am I? I am not qualified to initiate this action.** Moses questioned his qualifications and expressed his inadequacy in fulfilling the calling, saying "Who am I?" (Exodus 3:11). In response, God promised him His presence and gave him assurance that the mission would be successful. Moses focused on his limitations. The result was that he saw the inadequacy of *who* he thought he was. Since Moses identified himself with God, "You

have spoken to Your servant," an inside deeper assessment of He that was calling him would have transformed his perception to focus more on the unlimited God than himself. Nevertheless, the fear of his weakness was stronger than his courage!

2. **Suppose I go, and they ask your name? I lack the knowledge to initiate this action.** Moses wanted to be excused for his lack of knowledge in fulfilling the mission and not knowing even the name of God. "*What* would he tell the Children of Israel as *who* this God was?" (Exodus 3:13). Moses focused on *how* limited was his knowledge of God. In response, God told him who He was, who to talk to, and what to say, and gave him the assurance that the people would listen to him. God said, "I AM WHO I AM… thus you shall say to the children of Israel, 'I AM has sent me to you." (Exodus 3:14, NKJV). God wanted Moses to see *who* and *how* unlimited He was, and w*hat* the source and authority of Moses were.

3. **They will not believe me or listen to me: I do not believe I can initiate the action.** Moses doubted his ability and did not believe he had the power to fulfill the calling that God had told him to do. He did not believe that he could persuade the Children of Israel that God had actually appeared to him: "But suppose they will not believe me or listen to my voice; suppose they say, 'The LORD has not appeared to you.'" (Exodus 4:1, NKJV). Moses was apparently not willing to answer the call and wanted God to see *why* again focusing on his limited power. In response, God tried to increase his faith by showing him signs and the limitless power of *who* was sending him.

4. **I am slow in speech and tongue: This is not my calling to initiate.** Moses wanted to be excused because he lacked speaking and leadership abilities; therefore, this mission could not possibly be his calling, because he was not eloquent in speech. After excuses 1, 2, and 3, Moses, in excuse #4 told God that the call was not his. Refusing to join God in His work could appear, after all the signs, as distrust of God's ability to work with him. God desired that Moses' confidence and feelings of self-worth would come from his walk and relationship with Him: Moses said: "O my Lord, I am not eloquent, neither before nor since You have spoken to Your servant; but I am slow of speech and slow of tongue" (Exodus 4:10, NKJV). Moses now focused specifically on his vulnerabilities

CHAPTER 6
DEVELOPING INITIATION-ACTION

to show God *why* he was not qualified and *what* was limiting him. In response, God showed Moses that *whoever* made him is unlimited and able to recreate him. It must have been the best lecture of Moses' life: "*Who* has made man's mouth? Or *who* makes the mute, the deaf, the seeing, or the blind? *Have* not I, the LORD? Now therefore, go, and I will be with your mouth and teach you what you shall say". (Exodus 4:11-12, NKJV). God said He made him and that His power is unlimited to make him adequate.

5. **Please send someone else to do it; I do not want this call to initiate.** Even with the lecture God gave to Moses in Excuse #4, Moses did not want to fulfill the mission, because he was too afraid and unwilling to fulfill his calling and lead the people out of Egypt and asked God to send someone else to fulfill his calling. Although God had provided for all his excuses, Moses didn't want the assignment and did not want to take action to initiate the calling. He still did not believe in his self-worth, self-confidence, and vision for what the people were going through even though he knew them. Excuse #5 clearly revealed *wha*t was Moses' real motive, hidden, until now—by 'paralysis of the analysis', he did not want to be used for the initiation. In response, God provided Moses' brother, Aaron, and empowered Moses to use Aaron as his assistant and said, "And I will be with your mouth and with his mouth, and I will teach you *what* you shall do" (Exodus 4:14-15, NJKV).

Eventually, Moses submitted to the will of God to initiate the Exodus of the Children of Israel out of Egypt to the Promised Land. God originated the vision, but Moses was to walk with God to initiate and follow the process to completion. There is so much we can learn from this encounter. As leaders, we act the same way as Moses did, often very reluctant to take God for His word to obey Him. Moses focused all through this encounter on his inadequacy and was paralyzed by the fear of his limitations. Even when God showed him His unlimited power, Moses was still paralyzed by the fear of his limitations. This will happen to any leader-servant that sees the vision-purpose of God with a man's limited vision. Leaders or systems that fail to see the need for desired change or fail to respond to change often stagnate. Change is a dynamic function of time and has no respect for persons.

The case of Jonah is another classic example of a leader who clearly heard from God to take initiative to minister to the people of Nineveh. However, Jonah remained too stubborn to submit to God's directives (Jonah 2:10-3:10). He had to learn in a difficult way that initiative is a mark of Servant leadership. We often fail to trust God enough to believe that His grace is sufficient for us and that His power made perfect in those areas in which we find ourselves to be inadequate. To experience God in His strength and power, we must boldly step out in faith and obey Him, even in those things we think are impossible with man.

A CASE OF INITIATING A DESIRED CHANGE

When I accepted the job as the Dean for engineering diversity affairs, my charge from the senior dean was to initiate a new culture of change toward diversity, inclusion, and equity. As an engineer and scientist, I did not have any training in diversity management. In fact, until then, I never heard of the word diversity and equity and what they meant in higher education. It was not even well-defined in the dictionary at the time. Institutionally, the word or such office never existed. All I knew was that for 12 and half years in my education, I had received my engineering and physics education from three universities with four degrees and had not had a female or black professor or mentor. I did know, however, that some teachers could have benefited from cultural sensitivity education based on what I and others like me had experienced. So, the diversity and equity issues became a burden for me, and initiating a movement for change became a personal mission mandate. Hence, the position of dean for diversity affairs was more than a job but a dream opportunity to initiate the change I had wished for as a beginning point for service leadership.

My only guide at the time was Nehemiah's leadership principles on initiation. I strictly followed the four dimensions discussed above to formulate a framework for the initiation process. Through my own gut feelings and risk and enabled by being a tenured professor, I conceived a top-down service leadership approach to lead the change to a diverse and inclusive culture with which we (faculty, staff, students, and administration) were not familiar.

CHAPTER 6
DEVELOPING INITIATION-ACTION

The school's senior leadership raised diversity to one of five top priorities in its mission in line with quality in undergraduate and graduate education, excellence in research, and generating revenue. A task force was then created to study the current culture and climate and identify the desired change, key issues that needed to be addressed to influence the change and important areas on which to focus. With the report and recommendations, I proceeded to develop the strategic vision, mission, and value statements, focused on the key issues aligned with the school's other priorities, and identified people or created committees to work with me to formulate an action plan to follow. During implementation of the action-initiation stage, it was clear to me that people who at first resisted the initiation were either fearful of inclusion, as they did not quite understand what it all meant, some did not see the need for initiating such a broad-based diversity program and some did not know how to handle the differences. There was much missing or misinformation about diversity, and others simply were too complacent with the current culture or afraid that diversity would weaken the group's excellence. Today, the change took place and most of us, if not all, agree and celebrate the excellence and completeness that diversity is contributing to engineering education at the school.

Unlike the case of Moses, this is a case typical case of our leadership process today, where we create the vision and carry out all four stages of the initiation process. The key to its success is the courage to overcome your initial fears. My crucial driver of that courage was the passion to see the initiation as a personnel vision for a culture of inclusive excellence bigger than I and critical for the increased representation of my community in higher education. From the beginning, I saw the vision as a case like that of Nehemiah, who saw the vision of rebuilding the broken walls and gates in Jerusalem as a reproach on the people. In initiating the process, Nehemiah's invitation for action was focused, inspiring, and influential to the people; "Come and let us build the wall of Jerusalem, that we may no longer be a reproach" [Nehemiah 2:17, NKJV].

From these examples, we see that leaders lack the commitment to take action and initiatives for several reasons, including those summarized in Table 6.

Table 6: Reasons and associated issues for inaction to initiate

	Displayed reasons for inaction to initiate	Real (hidden) issue or why
1	Does not know how, what, why	Low motivation and commitment
2	Conflicts over who benefits the most	Self-centeredness
3	Excuses of past failures	Low self-will, self-determination
4	Unenthusiastic and resistance to change	Apathy, indifference, and shortsightedness
5	Sense of inadequacy and rejection	Low self-esteem and self-confidence
6	Fear of the unknown in the mission	Low self-confidence
7	Fear of the initiative by the leader	Sense of superiority and privilege
8	Threat and fear of being different	Prejudice and stereotype
9	Not enough support from others	Fear of over burden for the work
10	Someone else should originate it	Laziness and lack of leadership
11	Fear of failure to effect change	Lack of self-efficacy
12	Cannot see the need to act	Lack of vision and foresightedness
13	Sense of unwillingness	Fear of adversity and conflicts
14	Indecision and deferment on action	Fear of change or disobedience
15	Complacency with current state of things	Entitlement and socio-political correctness
16	Not understanding what is at stake	Sense of urgency or eagerness
17	The responsibility is not mine	Does not want to lead
18	Negative attitude and over analysis of action and outcome	Paralyzed by analysis and fear of failure
19	I want the change, but….	Do not really want the change
20	Avoids being a part of the initiative	Fear of legal repercussions

SUMMARY 6
DEVELOPING THE INITIATION-ACTION

Before starting this exercise, please read and follow the instruction in the preface of this workbook. Answers to these questions are contained in this chapter. Completion of these exercises after reading the chapter should take 60-90 minutes.

Discovering the Acts of Initiation ction
1. What is the role of Initiation-action as the final implementation stage of the initiation process
2. Why do leaders often give reasons for inaction to initiate a process of change?

Practicing the Acts of Initiation-Action
1. **Initiation-Action** is the final and implementation stage of the initiation process. It defines the action plan that fuses the other three stages of the final process.
   a. How do you understand the how, what, when, and why of the desired change?
   b. How did Moses, a servant of God, illustrates his struggles to for initiation-action
   c. What were Moses five excuses why he was not the one to initiate that process (Exodus 3:11, 4:1-15).
   d. The case of Jonah is another classic example of a leader who clearly heard from God to take initiative to minister to the people of Nineveh. (Jonah 2:10-3:10). What lesson did he lear?.
2. How is courage the key to success in initiation process
3. In initiating the process, Nehemiah's invitation for action was focused, inspiring, and influential to the people;. what was the impact of his call, "Come and let us build the wall of Jerusalem, that we may no longer be a reproach" [Nehemiah 2:17, NKJV].
4. What can we deduce from leaders lack the commitment to take action and initiatives
5. With reference to initiation leadership attribute, what take-away, meaning or lesson can you frame to improve your acts of initiation-action in a leadership process?
6. Write a personal commitment how to improve.

Topic Index

About This Book, 22
action-initiation
    definition, 71, 77
Affective Compassion, 67
authentic, 24, 26
authentic leadership, 37
Authentic Leadership, 45
Authenticity, 43
Comfort, 41
commitment, 19, 25
communication
    types of, 30
Communication, 30
Comparisons
    with other works, 40
Compassion, 28
credibility, 48
Desired Change, 55, 58, 60
Empathy-attribute, 28
focus, 55, 67, 71, 72, 75
Focus
    on vision purpose, 67, 69
    spiritually to act, 68, 69
    with passion, 67, 69
Focus-initiation
    definition, 67, 69
Foresightedness
    definition of, 55, 58, 60
Functional Definitions, 35
Influence
    Buy-in, 63, 65
    followers action, 63, 65
Influence–initiation
    definition, 55, 63, 64, 65
Initiative
    definition of, 29, 51, 52
inside-out, 46
Joshua, 19
law of, 42

LEADER, 28
Leader as Servant Leadership, 42
    definition, 25
Leader First., 23
Leader-as-Servant Leadership, 23
leader-servant's affection-attribute
    definition, 48
leadership, 25
Leadership Attributes, 43
leadership initiation-attribute
    definition of, 52, 55
Leadership Inner Value system, 25
Model, 23
Moses, 19
Moses' five excuses
    for inaction, 71, 77
Moses' five excuses
    for inaction, 71, 77
Navigation-attribute, 48
Personal Outward Authenticity, 47
process, 25
Reasons for inaction to initiate, 76
Servant, 23, 24
Teachable Moments to Grow, 69
test
    for leader-servant authenticity, 46
    of essential elements of personal
        authenticity, 46, 47
The Leadership Influence-attribute, 41
The Principle of Leadership
    Empathy-Attribute, 28
The Principle of Leadership
    Adaptability Attribute, 27
The Principle of Leadership
    listening-attribute, 30
vision-initiation, 52, 53, 57, 58, 59, 60
Vision-initiation
    definition, 57, 60

REFERENCES

[1]Greenleaf, R. (1970). *The Servant as Leader,* Indianapolis: The Robert K. Greenleaf Center

[2]Spears, L. (1996*).* "*Reflections on Robert K. Greenleaf and servant-leadership."* Leadership & Organization Development Journal, 17(7), 33-35

[3]Russell, R.F. (2001). "The role of values in servant leadership." *Leadership & Organization Development Journal,* 22(2), 76-83

[4]Russell, R.F., and Stone, A.G. (2002). "A review of servant leadership attributes: developing a practical model." *Leadership & Organization Development Journal,* 23(3), 145-15

[5]Terry. R. W (1993*).* **Authentic Leadership: Courage In Action*,* San Francisco, CA, Jossey-Bass

[6]George, B (2003). *Authentic Leadership: Rediscovering the Secrets to Creating Lasting Value.* San Francisco, CA, Jossey-Bass

[7]Shamir, B. & Eilam, G. (2005). "What's your story? Toward a life-story approach to authentic leadership." Leadership Quarterly, 16, 395–418.

[8]Anderson, GL (2009). *Advocacy Leadership: Toward a Post-Reform Agenda in Education*, Routledge, New York, 41

[9]Yacobi, B.G. *"Elements of Human Authenticity."* http://www.philosophytogo.org /wordpress/?p=1945, Retrieved, July 15, 2012

[10]George, B (2003). *Authentic Leadership: Rediscovering the Secrets to Creating Lasting Value*, San Francisco, CA, Jossey-Bass

[11]Wosu, SN (2014), *Leader as Servant Leadership Model*, Xulon Press

[12]Business dictionary .com

www.ingramcontent.com/pod-product-compliance
Lightning Source LLC
LaVergne TN
LVHW050025080526
838202LV00069B/6917